THAILAND

THAILAND
Published and distributed by:
Asia Books Co. Ltd.
5 Sukhumvit Soi 61, Sukhumvit Road
P.O. Box 11-40
Bangkok 10110, Thailand.
Tel: 3912680, 3910590
FAX N° (662) 38 11 621

© HOA-QUI Éditions
145, rue Saint-Dominique — 75007 Paris — France — 1989
© Éditions Xavier RICHER
1, quai aux Fleurs — 75004 Paris — France — 1989

Text : Christine ROUTIER LE DIRAISON

English translation : Mostyn MOWBRAY

Map page 12 : Dominique PARIS

Layout : Françoise TURK

Photographs : Patrick DE WILDE, with acknowledgements to:

Agence HOA-QUI : C. VAISSE, p. 15 (top), 26 (top right). E. VALENTIN, p. 27 (top left), 33, 48 (top), 88/89, 115, 119 (2), 120/121. M. RENAUDEAU, p. 26 (middle right), 83/83, 87. M. TRONCY, p. 37 (2).

Agence MAGNUM : B. BARBEY, p. 17. H. GRUYAERT, p. 24/25. M. RIBOUD, p. 54 (top). ABBAS, p. 47, 114 (top).

Agence RAPHO : LAUNOIS, p. 14, 18/19. P. KOCH, p. 20 (top). M. YAMASHITA, p. 21, 38 (bottom). A. DIAZ, p. 22 (top). N. WEELER, p. 42. HERMANN, p. 116, 122, 123.

Agence TOP : M. FRAUDREAU, p. 44/45. R. MAZIN, p. 78/79, 84/85. TIXADOR, P. 103.

Agence FOTOGRAM-STONE : p. 15 (bottom), 76, 96. H. KAYANAGH, p. 108. N. MACKENZIE, p. 112. KUSKAS, p. 118.

P. FRILET : p. 22 (bottom), 59, 66. M. MACINTYRE (ANA) p. 23 (b).

ISBN : 974-8206-52-1
PRINTED in SINGAPORE

THAILAND

Patrick DE WILDE
Christine ROUTIER LE DIRAISON

ASIA BOOKS

A land of singular charm

*S*pirituality and grace. In Thailand, most youths spend at least a few weeks of their life in a monastery. All girls learn the art of the dance, just as naturally as they learn to read and write. This perhaps explains, at least in part, the singularity of this enchanting kingdom which casts a spell of happiness and serenity over all who visit it. Thailand is literally a free country; the word itself means "the land of the free". Throughout its history, no foreign power has ever dominated it. Proud without being arrogant, devout without being bigoted, tolerant without being excessively permissive, it is a land of balanced proportions.

"Wait. From now on, life is to be lived calmly" said Paul Morand before he set foot on the soil of Thailand. From the deck of his ship, he saw its flat coastline as that of a country "beset by a flat calm which no breeze can dispel". His traveller's instinct was correct. At that time, at the beginning of the twentieth century, patience was still a virtue.

The Thai peasant waits for the rice to grow, the fisherman waits for the fish to bite, the monk waits for enlightenment and for detachment from the material world. Eternity is now. Tomorrow is yet to come.

This serenity, bordering at times on indolence, is the first thing that strikes Western visitors who, even on vacation, want things to be properly organized. For them, a train running late is a disaster, a missed appointment is a catastrophe, a change in the weather is a calamity. The Thais long ago decided to take things as they come. For them, life is divided into circumstances that are *sanuk* (pleasant) and *mai sanuk* (unpleasant). The same distinction applies to human beings, although it is obviously better not to be a mai sanuk person. The main purpose of existence is to avoid what is mai sanuk, or if not to make it sanuk. Simple!

Ephemeral beauty is among the pleasures of life: garlands of fragrant flowers patiently assembled to offer to Buddha or to a passing motorist; pyramids of fruit defying the laws of equilibrium; desserts wrapped in plaited banana leaves; vegetables carved like sculpted wood; statues in ice decorating a dinner-table... a paradoxical interpretation of Buddhism, which advocates detachment from the material things of this world, but a manner of endowing such material things with spiritual significance.

The elegance of bodily movement is also part of the art of living. Two Thais who meet greet each other graciously by raising their joined hands to their faces, sometimes accompanied by a light curtsy in the case of women. It is not done for people to have bodily contact in public; respect for others means respect for their bodies. Touching a person's head is a contemptuous act, for the head is considered to be the noblest part of the body.

The feet, however, are liable to get dirty, and it is ill-mannered to cross one's legs and point one foot in the other person's direction. Whether at home or in their places of worship, Thais always sit slightly askew, with their feet tucked behind them. Footwear is removed before entering a temple or a private house.

Pages 4-5: Gradually, the material from which the great statue of the reclining Buddha is made is transformed into precious metal. Monks and the faithful tirelessly apply extremely fine gold leaf, thereby acquiring merit for their next reincarnation.

Pages 6-7: Piety is inseparable from beauty. The Buddha is adorned with rare orchids, lotus flowers whose leaves are carefully folded, iridescent gold, and subtle perfumes, offered in a spirit of devotion and meditation.

Pages 8-9: Ephemeral beauty finds its highest expression in fêtes and festivals. These exquisite compositions are prepared for decorating the temple on the occasion of the ordination of a monk.

Opposite: The kinaris are mythological creatures, half women, half birds. They keep vigil in the Wat of the Emerald Buddha, gracious dancers frozen in immobility.

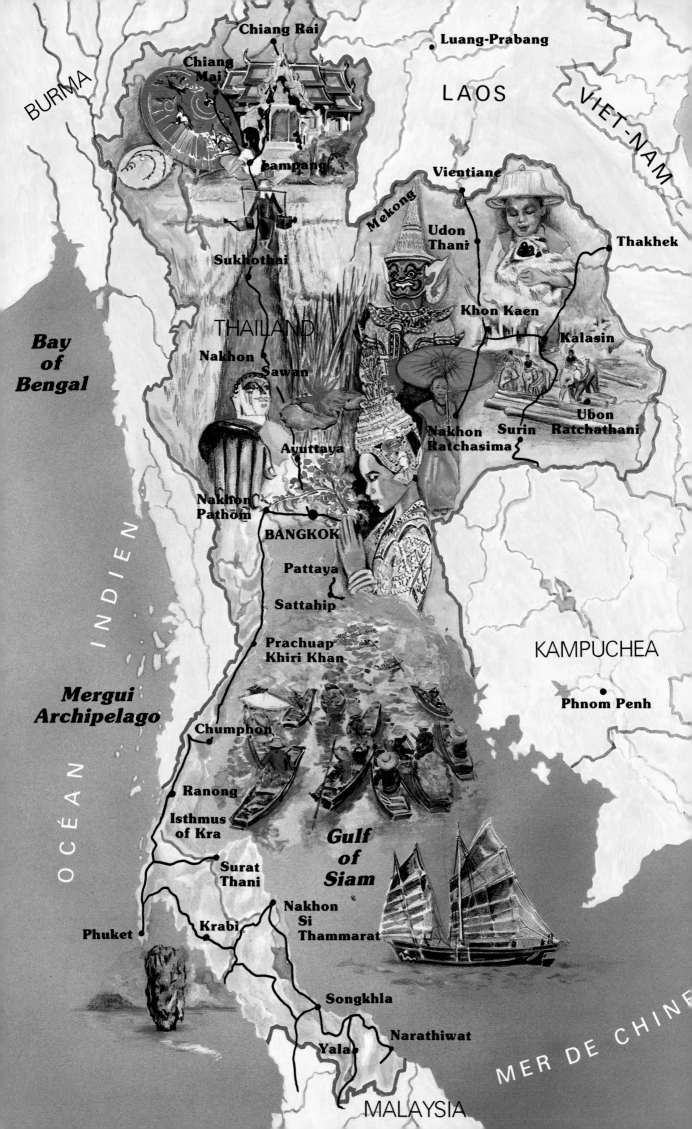

Far from being wearisome, tradition preserves everyone's personal security. The extended family is an established institution. Parents, children, grand-parents, uncles and cousins all live under the same roof and share their resources. Nobody is really alone, and even if far from his native village gathers a circle of friends whom he calls "father", "brother" or "sister" according to their age and the degree of respect in which he holds them. And everyone is taken care of in his or her old age; their children do not forget them or lose interest in them, and when the time comes they take their parents under their wing.

The King himself is a father-figure and is revered by all his subjects. Bumibhol Adulyadej, the ninth monarch of the Chakri dynasty, is the garantor of political stability in a constitutional monarchy which has survived intact since 1932. His consort, Queen Sirikit, combines beauty with nobility of spirit. The splendours of court life and the observance of protocol contrast with the simplicity and diligence of a ruler who is fully in touch with the realities of a country in which changes are occurring at an ever-increasing rate.

At the present time, 60% of the population are under twenty years old. Well-behaved schoolchildren in blue shorts and white shirts drink Coca-Cola and watch the same Japanese and American television series as their contemporaries in the West. Older youths wear blue jeans, ride motor-bikes and listen to disco music. Yet when the time comes they don a saffron robe, as their fathers and grandfathers did, and retire to a monastery for a few weeks or months. There is nothing remarkable in the fact that leading figures in the academic world have financed the construction of a place of worship and meditation on the campus of the University of Chieng Mai to placate the "forces of good".

Thailand conforms to the Buddhist calendar, and celebrated the year 2000 more than five hundred years ago. Most festivals are of religious or agricultural origin. The major events in the life of Buddha are celebrated: his birth, enlightenment, first sermon, and so on. The rice cycle gives rise to numerous fêtes and festivals: country fairs, games, cock-fights, music and dancing. The seasons and the phases of the moon are also occasions for rejoicing.

To celebrate the Thai New Year, which falls in April, the custom is to splash water on everyone you meet, including monks — and even statues. It is a purification rite, and it is no use trying to keep a low profile; you are bound to be the recipient of a forced shower, with the best of intentions!

In October and November comes Loy Krathong, the festival of light, transforming the country into a fairyland: thousands of tiny boats made from banana leaves, decorated with flowers and candles and perfumed with incense, are launched on the rivers and klongs in tribute to the goddess of water, the source of life and felicity in the kingdom of a million rice-fields.

The impact of Bangkok

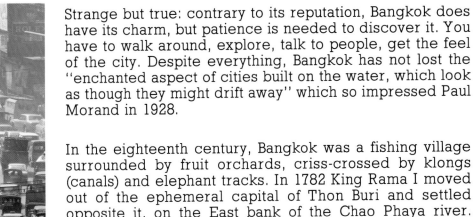

*T*he elephants have left, never to return. They abandoned Bangkok two centuries ago, like rats leaving a sinking ship, making way for 700,000 cars, 530,000 motorcycles, 130,000 trucks, 4,500 buses and 7,400 tuk-tuks (motor tricycles). Bangkok has no underground railway system. The former Venice of the East is an ecological nightmare from which the elephants escaped in good time. A hysterical frenzy of motor vehicles, bright lights, transistor radios and noise. What has happened to the charm of Bangkok?

Strange but true: contrary to its reputation, Bangkok does have its charm, but patience is needed to discover it. You have to walk around, explore, talk to people, get the feel of the city. Despite everything, Bangkok has not lost the "enchanted aspect of cities built on the water, which look as though they might drift away" which so impressed Paul Morand in 1928.

In the eighteenth century, Bangkok was a fishing village surrounded by fruit orchards, criss-crossed by klongs (canals) and elephant tracks. In 1782 King Rama I moved out of the ephemeral capital of Thon Buri and settled opposite it, on the East bank of the Chao Phaya river. Bangkok had begun its inevitable expansion. Two years later, the first road was built — it is still called New Road although it is the oldest thoroughfare in the capital.

The Chinese community has played a major role in the rapid development of Bangkok, and indeed until quite recently its Chinatown was the business centre of the city. Business of all kinds, from noodle trading to banking.

Above: The traditional rickshaw cycle has been relegated to the provinces of Thailand, squeezed out by the frenzy of urban life in Bangkok. Traffic congestion in the capital has attained colossal proportions, and poses an almost insoluble problem for the municipal authorities.

Opposite: 46 metres long and 15 metres high, the Reclining Buddha of Wat Po is the largest in Thailand. Its position symbolizes access to Nirvana.

Too bad for those who hanker after the old teak buildings; concrete has taken over. It is not wise for a Bangkokian, as an inhabitant of the capital is called, to stay away from his neighbourhood for too long, or he may find it unrecognizable when he returns. Shopping centres, banks, condominiums and big hotels spring up, ever higher, in the space of a few months. The future World Trade Center will be twenty floors higher than the 43-floor Baiyoke Tower in the Patrunam quarter. Who remembers the time when Bangkok's buildings were shaded by coconut palms?

With a population estimated at between 6 and 7 million, the capital of Thailand is forty-five times the size of the second city of the country, Nakhon Ratchasima. How many of Bangkok's street vendors, dockers, labourers, barmaids and tuk-tuk drivers succumbed to the lure of the big city, believing it to be preferable to working in the rice-fields?

But, strange as it may seem, Bangkok is a city of country people. The outward trappings of modernity conceal a way of life deeply rooted in tradition. The leaden mantle of loneliness has not yet descended on the capital of Thailand. Even — and indeed especially — in the smallest homes, room can always be found for a cousin from the provinces who has decided to try his luck in the big city.

The serenity of Buddha still reigns in what was once Krungthep, the City of the Gods. It suffices to cross the threshold of a wat to forget the urban tumult. There are at least four hundred such temples; some of them are royal, like that of the Emerald Buddha, others are small neighbourhood temples nestling among banyan and frangipani trees, oases of gold and saffron conducive to rest and meditation.

Above: The Golden Mountain, the highest point in Bangkok, is only 80 metres high. The capital's skyline is now dominated by modern high-rise buildings.

Opposite: Behind crenellated ramparts rise the temple spires and varnished roofs, decorated with stylized serpents, of the old Royal City.

Preceding double page: The maintenance and renovation of the temples are a permanent concern of Buddhists, who in performing this work acquire merit. To retouch the prangs of the Arun Wat, 79 metres above the city, it is preferable to have a good head for heights.

Opposite: Though the King of Thailand no longer travels by elephant, he has adopted an equally dignified British form of transport.

Above, left: Young Thais have a taste for uniforms and a sense of discipline. Schoolboys in navy blue and white, and scouts in khaki, are always impeccably attired.

Above: The River Chao Phaya, which irrigates the ricefields of Thailand, is also Bangkok's major traffic artery. Trains of barges, water-taxis, canoes, floating shops and houseboats all give rise to permanent activity.

Early risers are rewarded: every morning, in the half-light of dawn, the monks collect their day's food from the faithful. Like a vision of electric yellow and orange colours, they invest the city in silence and meditation. At the same time, women and children begin to weave garlands of jasmins which will be sold at street intersections and in temples, as offerings of ephemeral beauty.

The barmaids and masseuses are still asleep. Bangkok is ridding itself of its nocturnal fug. Vendors in canoes have already set out to sell their wares on the klongs. The klongs, too, are victims of modernization; they are being filled in one by one, transformed into streets, avenues and motorways. Meanwhile Bangkok is sinking into the water even more rapidly than Venice, like a megalopolis punished by the gods for having wanted too much too quickly.

Left: There are plenty of restaurants serving tasty dishes. The Thais eat at all hours of the day, and meals are generally informal.

Top Left: Americán soft drinks have become popular, and young children acquire a taste for Coca-Cola at an early age.

Above: Grocery shops and other stores are often family businesses. In the older parts of the city, the shopkeepers live on the premises and the point of distribution is close to the point of production.

Right: At dusk, on the terrace of the Oriental Hotel, the ghost of the Venice of the East seems to emerge from the past. The Oriental offers the most romantic view over the River Chao Phaya in the whole of Bangkok.

Overleaf: Chinatown, in the heart of old Bangkok, has lost none of its appeal. Here are still to be found calligraphers and seal engravers who have not forgotten the art of the ideogram.

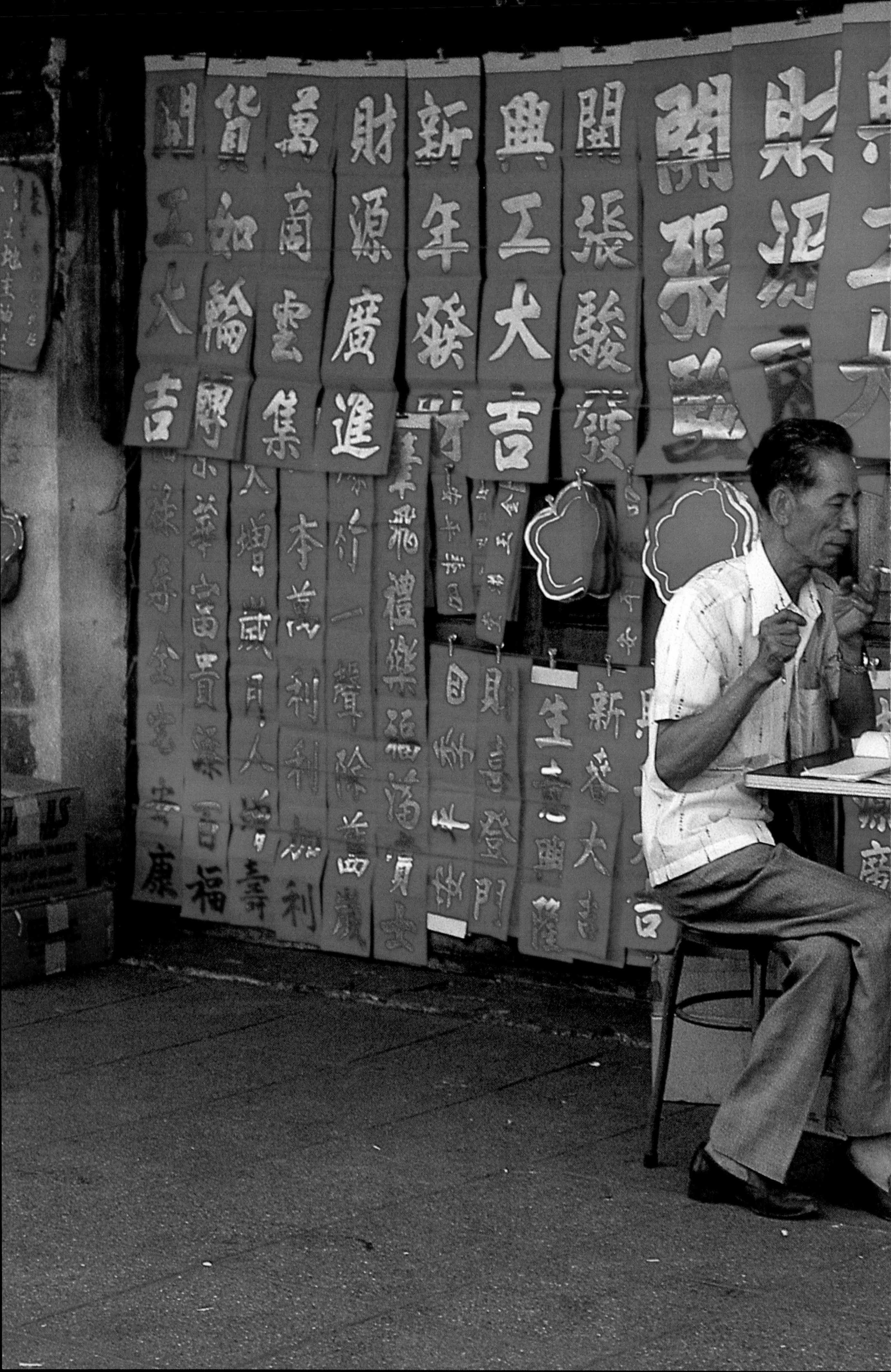
開工大吉
萬商雲集
財源廣進
新年發財
興工大吉
生意興隆
新春大吉

The market is a pleasure-ground for everyone: vendors, shoppers and strollers. The merchandise is attractively displayed, and even this flower-girl matches the colour of her blouse with that of her flowers. Food vendors, too, take pains with their colour-shemes. Here, plastic packaging has not replaced banana-leaves.

The empire of the senses

*T*he Bangkokians are not bored on Sundays. There is nothing more *sanuk* than strolling around the weekend market. Too bad that since the bicentenary festivals in 1982 it has moved from the majestic setting of Sanam Luang and is now out in the Northern suburb of Suan Chatuchak; it is still the favourite destination of family outings.

The country folk arrive with their pole-baskets full of treasures from the jungle, grain, spices and dried fish. All the shopkeepers in the city and its suburbs have stalls in the market. Saturdays and Sundays are supermarket days, with every conceivable kind of merchandise on sale: wickerware, transistors, tropical fish, textile fabrics, rare orchids, Chinese soup, German shepherd dogs, baby pythons, ball-point pens, portraits of the King, parrots, coconuts, amulets... you name it, they have it!

Workers, bonzes, housewives, schoolchildren and tourists browse among the stalls, assailed at every step by different fragrances and tempted by the merchandise on sale. In April, the children bring out their kites and stage contests under the leadership of their elders. Inveterate gamblers gather around a bowl in which two fish fight to the death, or bet on the outcome of a combat between a snake and a mongoose.

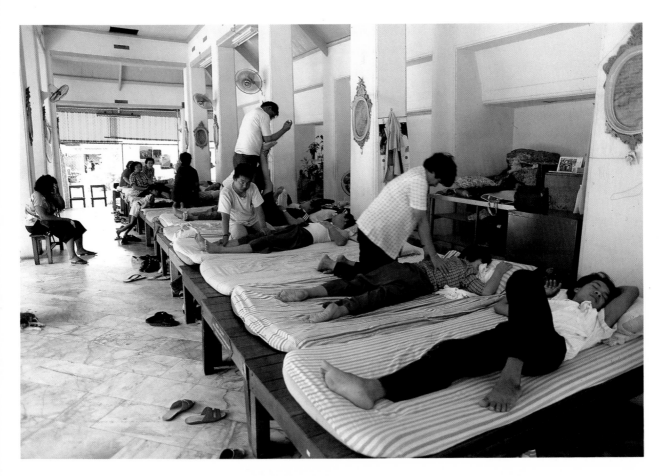

Above: Thai massage gained its patents of nobility long before the young ladies of Patpong. It is a long-established skilled craft far removed from its present-day less reputable connotations.

Opposite: Urban posters are often hand-painted by commercial artists. Here, one of them puts the finishing touches to a portrait of His Majesty King Bumibhol.

This popular market is the most spectacular one among many others in Bangkok. In the Bangrak market shoppers can choose their day's menu from among a profusion of vegetables, piled high in precariously-balanced pyramids, skewered meat of all kinds, and bowls of meng da, a species of water-beetle highly prized as an ingredient in sauces so hot they would burn the tongue of the devil himself. Not to mention a variety of exotic fruits: mangosteens, dark red apples, jambhu, Java plums, lamut, bitter-sweet mangoes, and spiky rambutans.

Those in search of flowers go to the banks of the Krung Kasem klong, where orchids are on sale in the shade of the flame-trees. On the opposite bank, coconuts gathered by the monkeys of Samui are heaped in special baskets, graded by size.

In front of the Rachanada Wat, opposite the Golden Mountain, the Bangkok shop for amulets which they believe can protect them from various risks, including illness, sterility, adultery, gunshot wounds, traffic accidents... every amulet has its own virtues.

Even at night, there are markets, lit by storm lamps, where one can sample tasty seafood on the spot, along with the local spirit Mekong, the poor man's whisky!

Above: Classical Thai dances demand a mastery of bodily movement that is learned at a very early age. Most Thai girls are able to bend their wrists in expressive gestures and know the significance of every position of the hands.

Left: Young dancers relaxing. Performances of lakhon (classical dances) and khon (masques) can last for several hours. The repertory is derived from mythology and from the Hindu sagas of Ramayana and Mahabharata.

Life on the klongs

*T*he klongs are no longer silent. One of the favourite sports of local youths is zigzaging at speed among the other boats and water-taxis in hang-yao, a craft powered by a truck engine, with a transmission shaft which also serves as a rudder. The hang-yao is to the klongs what the motorcycle is to the streets: a fast and noisy means of getting around.

The klongs are as much a part of the folklore of Bangkok as the canals are of the folklore of Venice. But they are also of economic and social importance in a country which is criss-crossed by more than three million kilometres of waterways. Despite the fact that many klongs have been, and are still being, filled in, Bangkok is still riddled by a network of klongs, and it is possible (almost) to reach Don Muang International Airport by boat.

In the villages of the central plain, the people still live in dwellings built on piles over the water, a survival of a long tradition of amphibious existence. The klong serves as a street, a sewer, a place to wash in, and a source of fish. In the face of all conventional principles of health, hygiene and ecology, the water of these canals seems to serve these multiple purposes, though how it does so is a mystery. In Thailand, people wash, just as they eat, when they feel the need for it; there is no fixed schedule. Both activities are among the pleasures, as well as the necessities, of life.

For many villages, the klongs are the only means of communication with the outside world. The men drive their motorboats, while the women negotiate the traffic-jams of the floating markets in rowing boats.

Following page: One hour by road from Bangkok, the floating market of Damnoen Saduak is a survival of old-time Siam. The women vendors leave their villages very early in the morning to reach the market via a labyrinth of canals winding through tropical vegetation.

Left: These large earthenware jars, decorated with dragons, are of Chinese origin. They are placed on terraces where they serve as a reserve of drinking water.

Right: On land and water alike, there are always vendors of tasty comestibles to eat on the spot or to take away.

At peak hours, the klongs of Bangkok are a hive of shopping activity. Housewives cast an eye over the waterborne vendors from their balconies and place their orders. Though they have moved out from the centre to the outskirts of the city, these floating markets are still a feature of the local scene.

The best-known of them is the Damnoen Saduak market, held every morning. Every boat has a different cargo: pyramids of pineapples, mountains of water-melons, wickerware, pottery... there are even floating restaurants. Here and there one encounters a boatload of monks, whose orange robes countrast with the blue shirts of the peasants and the multicoloured merchandise on sale.

After the boats have dispersed, the klongs become the playground of children who plunge naked in the wakes of the hang-yaos. Most of them have learned to swim almost as soon as they could walk. Perhaps they were fishes in a previous life!

Above: Thai anglers use nets in the form of giant butterflies. In this country, fish — along with rice — is the staple diet, and is netted everywhere, even in the ricefields.

Left: The klongs and rivers are favourite playgrounds for children, who are indifferent to the cleanliness of the water.

Right: The Buddhist religion respects all animals, and the natural environment brings children into contact with all species. Who could wish for a more lovable companion than the one pictured here?

70% of all arable land in Thailand (9 million hectares) is given over to the cultivation of rice. Agriculture is not mechanized to any significant extent, and much of the peasant's work is hard manual labour. Most of them do not own the land which they cultivate.

Rural Thailand

O n the map, Thailand looks like the profile of an elephant's head, the ear outlined by 1,000 kilometres of the course of the Mekong and the trunk extending down to Malaysia.
It is a land of peasants, fishermen and mountain-dwellers, covering an area approximately equal to that of France. Its landscape features rectangular rice-fields, dense jungles peopled by gibbons, majestic and mysterious mountains, quiet valleys through which flow rivers and klongs, cathedral-like forests of hevea, broad tranquil rivers, austere grasslands where the last vestiges of the Khmer Empire are fast disappearing, palm-fringed beaches, lakes dotted with lotus... over all of which Buddha smiles. Far from the frenzy of Bangkok, life proceeds changelessly in the mubans (rural communities) of Thailand, where 65% of the country's population still live.

Thai villages are traditionally located on river banks; the
houses are built on piles to protect them from floods,
maurauding animals, reptiles and insects. Rigour and
simplicity are the keynotes: the frames of the dwellings
are in teak and bamboo, the walls are made of plaited
straw, and the roof is a canopy of leaves. Inside, there is
practically no furniture; the people sleep on mats which
they unroll at day's end. The only decoration is a picture
of the royal family pinned to the wall alongside a calendar
and a photograph of the son who has gone off to work for
the monks or for a Chinese grocer.

Life is organized around the rice cycle, beginning at the
end of March, the hottest time of the year. The labourer,
inseparable from his buffalo, cuts the first furrows in which
the new seeds are planted. After planting, the rice-fields
are flooded from the complicated network of irrigation
canals laid out centuries ago and ceaselessly maintained.

The scene becomes a succession of mirrors reflecting the sky as far as the eye can see.

Gradually, the young shoots emerge, and when the seedlings are planted out everyone is in the fields; children stay away from school, women desert the market, and men assume an authoritative air befitting the occasion. The shoots are assembled into tight bundles ready for planting out. It is a tiring job, and there is hardly time to recover from it before the harvest comes around.

At the end of the rainy season, the youths who have spent a period of time in the monastery return home. While their hair and eyebrows — shaven according to custom — grow again, the rice comes to maturity. The harvest is a joyful occasion, after which the paddy has to be dried before threshing commences. For thirty million Thais, rice is not only their staple diet, it is also their livelihood.

Chinese cooks are ducks' worst enemies. Many restaurants, especially in Bangkok, are frequented by lovers of glazed duck, and even the bird's tongue is highly appreciated.

Carefree children happily fish in the ditches, pools and canals with large nets in the shape of giant butterflies. Will they be farmers or fishermen when they grow up? The question hardly arises in Thailand, where fish is the inseparable accompaniment to rice. So long as there is rice in the paddy and fish in the water, no-one need worry.

Rural existence is enlivened by simple pleasures: listening to the news from another planet, called Bangkok, on the radio; the admission of a son to the monastery; shopping in the market; gossiping; having fun on fête days; hoping to win the National Lottery.

No-one neglects his duties to the bonzes in the wat, nor must one forget to placate the phis, the invisible and capricious spirits who preside over the destiny of human beings. Every family regularly makes offerings of flowers and food to these spirits in a miniature temple built on piles.

Salt is extracted from the salt marshes in the vicinity of Bangkok. The workers wear protective masks which give them a fobbidding appearance; they can be encountered between Samut Sakhon and Samut Songkhran.

But the phis are not always grateful. In the poorest areas, such as the North-East, there is a great temptation to try one's luck in Bangkok, even if it might mean jumping out of the frying-pan into the fire.

Under the smile of Buddha

*T*here was once a Prince named Siddharta, for whom the soothsayers foretold an extraordinary destiny. Despite the luxury surrounding him, he was not happy. One day, walking in the forest, he discovered the four afflictions of existence: illness, old age, poverty and death. After many years of wandering and privation he discovered the four noble truths: pain, the origin of pain, the cessation of pain, and the way to the cessation of pain. This happened on the borders of Nepal in the sixth century B.C. Buddha, the person who received enlightenment, was to have a profound impact on the heart and soul of Asia. After becoming established in the Indian sub-continent from Kashmir to Ceylon, Buddhism spread rapidly through South-East Asia from the tenth century onwards, and gained a firm footing in Thailand.

Officially, 90% of the population of Thailand adhere to the Buddhist religion, which is called Therevada, meaning "Little Vehicle". It is more than a religion, it is a state of mind, a conception of life which influences every moment of existence. The distinguishing features of Buddhism are its tolerance, its fatalism and its sense of proportion. It is full of nuances; it is like a zither with three strings, which break if they are over-stretched and produce dissonant music if they are not sufficiently tightened.

Images of Buddha, in jasper, gold, bronze, stone, wood or stucco, cast their oblique gaze over the whole of Thailand. Their privileged place is the wat, but every home has its own statue of Buddha. It is "leased" from a craftsman or a factory, because the revered image cannot be sold. The statue materializes the presence of the Master among human beings, and supernatural powers are vested in it. Ordering a statue of Buddha also enables a person to acquire merit, and ensures a better reincarnation.

The monk wears a long one-piece robe which stays in place without buttons or clips. Putting it on is an art that is learned at an early age. All children who attend monastery schools must wear this garb.

51

Sticks of incense burn at all times in the temples, in homage to Buddha. Certain statues are draped in a length of saffron fabric to denote their sacred nature. The atmosphere is conducive to meditation, and shoes must be removed before entering.

The representation of Buddha is strictly codified in canonical texts, in terms of symbolic attitudes and distinguishing features. There are 32 principal distinguishing features and 80 secondary ones; for example, the hairs grow one by one, the skin is delicately smooth, he has forty teeth, his taste is supremely refined, he has a divine voice like melodious birdsong.

In the Thai iconography, there are 40 conventional attitudes plus a whole range of gestures evoking the different stages of the life of Buddha. The most frequent attitude is that of the hero (Virasana: legs folded one under the other). But one also encounters Buddha calling the earth to witness his enlightenment, Buddha preaching his first sermon, Buddha settling family quarrels, Buddha sleeping, and so on.

Above: Early every morning the monks collect their food for the day from the local people, who thereby acquire merit.

Opposite and right: Much of the monks' day is spent studying sacred texts. In rural areas, the monastery serves as a public school, which explains the close links between the village and the wat.

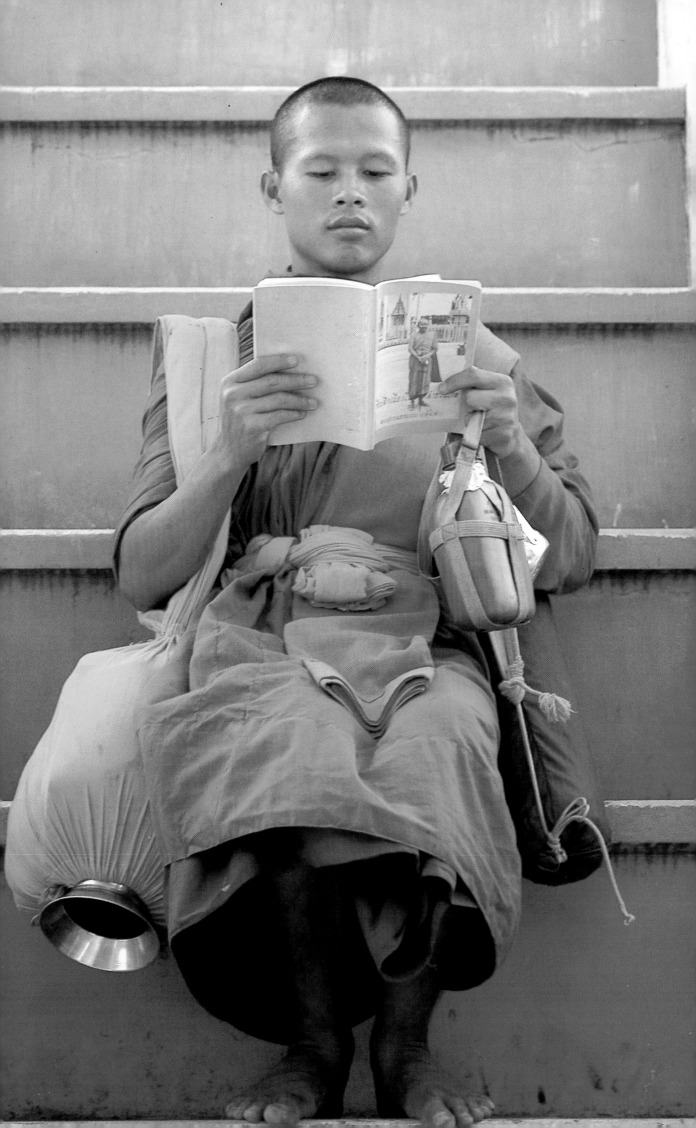

Devotion and harmony are the keynotes in all Thailand's 26,000 wats. Somerset Maugham wrote of them : "It makes you laugh with delight to think that anything so fantastic could exist on this somber earth". The wat is more than a place of worship; it is a place of culture and a gathering-place, serving at one and the same time as a school, a festival hall, a public park, and a salon. Each part of the building has a specific function: the bot (main chapel), the chedi (reliquary), the ho raking (belfry housing the gong), the library, the monks' living quarters, the sala (shelter for pilgrims).

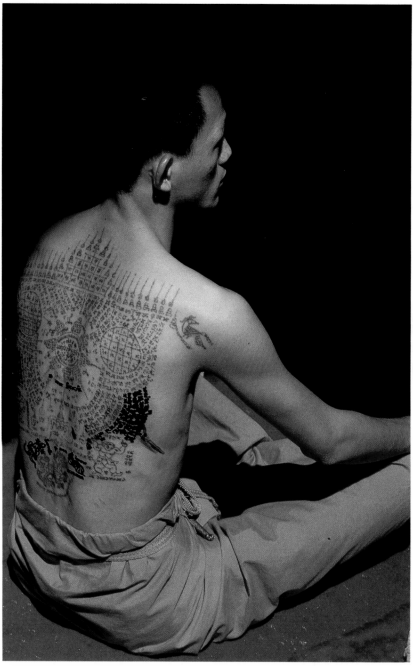

Left and below: Tattoos have religious significance; they protect people from danger and from evil influences. Men engaged in high-risk occupations usually have themselves tattooed.

Right: The monks eat together in the sala, an open-sided pavilion which also serves as a dormitory for passing visitors.

In the wat, the monks stroll around, meditate, study, chant, smoke, wash their laundry, and tend the garden. Nearly 13,000 people in Thailand wear the saffron robe, if not for life at least for a few months. Every male who is a practising Buddhist is required to be temporarily ordained in order to perfect his religious education and to enable his family to acquire merit. This temporary retreat takes place in the monsoon months.

The monastic life is governed by 227 rules. The novice undertakes to respect all forms of life (including insect life), to refrain from lying and stealing, to remain chaste, and to possess no money of his own. But this is by no means all; he is not allowed to smell flowers, burn wood, perfume himself, whistle or sing, sleep in a soft bed, touch silver, sit with legs outstretched, gamble... the list of interdictions is a long one.

It goes without saying that monks take a vow of poverty. Their possessions are confined to three jackets, a begging bowl, a needle, a belt, and a strainer (to avoid inadvertently swallowing a living creature).

The population must provide the monks (who in many cases are children) with food. In return, the sangha (the monastic community) maintains harmony among all human beings. The monks care for bodily and spiritual needs, and their serenity in this day and age is truly amazing. Nothing surprises them, even being asked to officiate at the opening of a new bank.

Above: The wat is an essentially masculine domain. A few women, generally widows or the victims of misfortune, retire there. They dress in white and shave their heads.

Right: The ordination of novices can be an impressive ceremony, as at Mae Hong Son, near the Burmese frontier. After parading for three days in a princely costume, this young boy will be ordained as a monk.

Overleaf: Lay Buddhists spend a studious retreat in the centre of meditation at Dhammakaya.

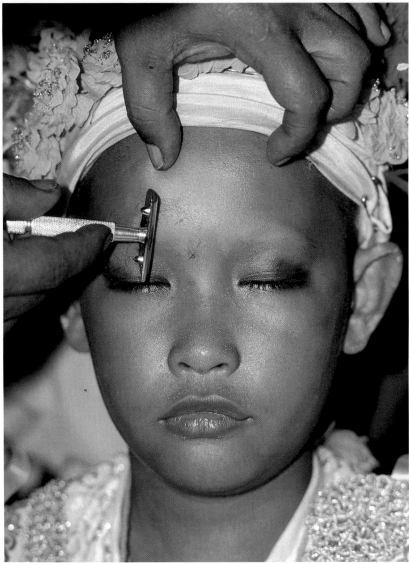

The fête of Poi Sang Long, held at Mae Sariang prior to the rainy season, marks the provisional ordination of novices. Postulants are carried around the town on men's shoulders for three days; they must not set foot on the ground except in front of the temples, where they exchange their bright costume for the saffron robe and have their heads and eyebrows shaved.

The empire builders

*U*nbeknown to Saint Louis, the King of France, while he was on the throne things were happening in a distant part of the world; the first Siamese State was emerging. Sukhothai (the word means "the dawn of felicity") was rising from the jungle, with its palaces, pagodas, Buddhist statutes of ethereal grace, lotus-covered pools, sumptuous court life, and happy peasants and craftsmen.

In 1328, Angkor, 466 kilometres North of Bangkok (which at that time was a tiny village nobody had ever heard of) was in rapid decline, and the Thais, a rice-growing people who had moved down from the South of China, had had enough of Khmer domination.

For this part of the world, this counts as recent history when we remember that South-East Asia was the cradle of the world's earliest Bronze Age civilization 5,600 years ago. However, if Sukhothai was so important for the Siamese it was because it marked the emergence of a nation in a land which until then had been a juxtaposition of small kingdoms incessantly at war with one another.

But war was not the only pastime of the kings and their nobles. They liked wearing silk clothes, eating from fine dishes and living in huge palaces among obsequious courtiers, surrounded by temples containing statues of Buddha in gold, jasper, bronze and stone.

Every kingdom contributed to the art and architecture of this part of the world; Dvaravati (VIth to XIth centuries), of predominantly Indian influence; Srivijaya (VIIIth to XIIth centuries), which originated in Indonesia and spread to Southern Thailand; Lopburi (VIIth to XIVth centuries), of Khmer derivation; Lan Na (XIIth to XXth centuries), specific to Northern Thailand and with Burmese and Laotian influences; and U Thong (XIIth to XVth centuries), of a more specifically Thai character. The Bangkok style (Rattanakosin) came later, only two centuries ago.

Opposite: The Buddha of the Sra Se Wat at Sukhothai is reflected in the lotus-covered lake. Sukhotai is reflected in the lotus-covered lake. Sukhotai was the capital of Thailand from 1257 to 1379, and is a spot of major historic interest.

Top right: This bas-relief in the Pimai museum is in the Lopburi style. It symbolizes the accession to Nirvana, and depicts meditating Buddhas who have resisted the temptations of the flesh, symbolized by diabolical dancers.

Sukhothai reached its apotheosis under King Ram Khamheng (1275-1317), who invented Thai writing and had his own idea of happiness: "Fortunate is the city of Sukhothai; the water abounds in fish, rice flourishes in the fields... trade in elephants is unrestricted". In this paradise, no taxes were levied and one could request a personal audience with the King to discuss one's little problems. It was too good to last.

When the great King died, the kingdom split up into several small states. At the end of the XIVth century Sukhothai became a vassal state of Ayutthaya, ruled over by greedy princes, 400 kilometres downstream on the Chao Phaya river.

Top left: The gold leaf applied to Buddhas is so fine that it takes years to cover a statue.

Above: This candle-holder in the shape of a royal barge receives candles offered by the faithful.

Right: This colossal seated Buddha in the Si Chum Wat in Sukhotai is 15 metres high. Its head is reached via a staircase concealed in the wall.

The city of thirty-three rulers had nothing to envy of Sukhothai. At the time, Siam entered its golden age: architecture, sculpture, painting and literature flourished. Ayutthaya itself, which had a population of a million, was a cosmopolitan megalopolis with thousands of foreign residents, including a Japanese colony, and with Portugese and French churches. Louis XIV of France established an Embassy there during the reign of King Narai in 1662, headed by the elegant Chevalier de Chaumont, who must have regretted his wig and his heavy brocade clothing.

But over the sumptuous life of the court there loomed the shadow of the battlefield; the kingdom waged incessant wars against the Khmers and the Burmese. In 1767, after two years of siege, Ayutthaya fell to the Burmese army. The city was sacked, its treasures burned, and desolation reigned in what had been a radiant capital. The Thais never forgave the victors for its ruthless destruction.

Two years later, the Siamese once more acquired a King and an ephemeral capital: Thonburi, opposite Bangkok on the right bank of the Menam river.
In 1782 a new King crossed the river, set up home in Bangkok, and founded the Chakri dynasty. He was Rama I.

The good life was resumed, and gradually, as the artistic heritage of Siam was reconstituted, the country began to enter the modern world, ruled by sovereigns who successfully preserved their people from colonization.

Left: This temple door at Pimai, in Eastern Thailand, is an example of the monumental rigour of Khmer architecture.

Right: The temple of Muang Tham, in the province of Buri Ram, was built between the Xth and XIth centuries in the classical style of Angkor. It was originally constructed as a palace for a Khmer king.

Elephants in the teak forests

*N*orthern Thailand is noted for its craftsmen, its elephants, and its sticky rice. It is a mountainous region, and has retained its singularity despite the unification of the country. Its Golden Triangle, where the frontiers of Thailand, Burma and Laos meet, was a magnet to the last adventurous explorers of the remotest parts of Asia. The North cultivates superlatives like other areas cultivate rice and coconuts: it has the most beautiful girls, the finest temples, the most skilled craftsmen, the most joyous fêtes and festivals, the most majestic scenery, and the oddest people.

The most pleasant way of setting out from Bangkok to explore the North is via the River Chao Phaya. In three hours the boat reaches Ayutthaya, the city of thirty-three kings, surrounded by water as it was once surrounded by Burmese warriors. It is the starting point for a nostalgic and fascinating journey through buffalo and elephant country.

The buffalos live among the rice-fields, the elephants in the forest. What were formerly capitals, now fallen from their ancient glory, mount guard over the invisible frontier separating the North from the central plain: Kamphaeng Phet, Sukhothai and Sri Satchanalai. If the jungle has spared them, Buddha is surely responsible, for here nature reigns supreme.

After Chieng Mai, the transverse roads lead nowhere; they stop at closed frontiers which only smugglers and guerillas risk crossing. The mountains are inhabited by tribes and the forests by elephants. The rivers Ping, Wang, Yom, Nan and Kok — names that sound like a roll-call of Asiatic schoolchildren! — flow through fertile valleys where strawberries grow.

In the teak forests, elephants who have been trained for the job for six years gather and stack logs. 20,000 of them have been trained for this task in the State-owned forests, and they have the status of privileged civil servants: three days on, three days off, three months' holiday a year, and retirement at the age of 60.

Left: This bamboo footbridge in the province of Tak crosses the shallow waters of a lake whose level is controlled by the Bumibhol Dam.

Top, and following page: The elephants trained to work in the teak forests are given a daily bath to refresh them after their labours.

Top left: Rice is cultivated in irrigated paddies in the valleys of the North. A special variety which does not need to grow in water is cultivated at higher altitudes.

Bottom left: A pilgrim monk walking barefoot in the countryside.

Bottom right: Slender liana bridges are still to be encountered in the jungle.

Above: A landscape in the North seen through the early morning mist.

Following double page: The elephants shower themselves with their trunks when ordered to do so. The Karnaks take advantage of bath-time to examine their elephants and make sure that they have received no injury while working.

Double page 84-85: A young woman of the Lisu tribe chatting with an acrobatic monkey.

On the Mae Sariang road leading to the Burmese frontier one may expect at any time to encounter these forestry workers, under the authoritative direction of a Karen mahout (these people have no equal as elephant trainers). The Burmese influence is evident in Northern Thailand, where the women wear Burmese-style diagonally-buttoned tunics and where the temple architecture is directly derived from the former Pegu style (now called Pagan). Trade in precious stones flourishes, and the traveller is tempted to look for the celebrated Magok rubies in the innumerable jewellers' shops that resemble grocery stores. To the North, in the direction of the Golden Triangle, is the River Kok, where tourists can experience the thrill of shooting the rapids aboard a long-hulled canoe, without the slightest danger, for they are quite modest rapids. This river is the principal line of communication with the outside world.

Not far away is the legendary River Mekong, which here marks the frontier, unfortunately closed. When the river enters Laos it is still a wild and capricious mountain torrent; it has another 4,335 kilometres to flow, in the course of which it acquires its true character.

Half-way to the sea, the Mekong is already 10 kilometres wide. Its serenity in the dry season is misleading; it can become very rough indeed, overflow its banks and sweep away everything in its path.

Dozing beside the Mekong, like a dilapidated palace of the opium barons, Chieng Saen is a spot where the magic of the great river can be experienced to the full. The mist-shrouded outline of the opposite bank seems to be steeped in mystery for all time.

Dragons and other marvels

*E*lephants are intelligent creatures. Remember that as you climb the 306 steps up to the Phra That Doi Suthep Wat, the most celebrated temple of Chieng Mai, built on a hilltop 11 kilometres from the town in the fourteenth century. The site was chosen by a white elephant assigned by King Kuena to seek a suitable spot for the enshrinement of a relic of Buddha. The elephant's choice was a wise one. The view is magnificent, taking in the city of Chieng Mai lying on either side of the River Ping, which is dotted with islands of greenery. A few tall buildings testify to the city's recent prosperity (mainly due to tourism), and its old teak houses and low-eaved temples nestle amid the vegetation. The old part of the city is clearly distinguishable, enclosed in a rectangle bordered by moats.

Founded in 1296 by King Ram Kamhaeng and Mengrai, ruler of the kingdom of Lan Na, Chieng Mai was the capital of the region's first independent kingdom. Its situation enabled it to maintain close links with the kingdom of Luang Prabang (Laos). For two centuries, from 1556 to 1775, it was under Burmese domination. Until 1920, the city was accessible only by river or on elephant-back.

The best way to get your bearings is to take a trip by rickshaw cycle. There is no need to establish an itinerary, and in any case the driver will arrange it to suit himself, so that the trip ends at a shop owned by one of his cousins or a restaurant run by a close friend.

A visit to the historic centre is a must. Enchantment begins as soon as you pass through the Gate of the White Elephant, which formerly served as a look-out point for the approach of Burmese or Laotian enemies. Chieng Mai has more than a hundred temples, whose architecture reveals Mon and Burmese influences. They contain treasures of lacquer and gold, enamel and coral, carved wood and bronze. Silence reigns in these tranquil wats shaded by banyan trees and frangipani. Bare feet tread the cool floor-slabs soundlessly. The living quarters of the monks are bedecked with large draperies whose colours range from bright yellow to dark red. There is nothing stressful about the cultural sightseeing tour.

Making parasols is a traditional craft in the village of Bo Sang in the North. The ribs are of bamboo, and over them is laid a hand-painted paper of vegetable origin.

Following double page: The architecture of the temples in the North, especially in Chieng Mai, is characterized by a marked Burmese influence. The roofs, decorated with nagas, slope down almost to the ground, and the carved wood façades are richly decorated.

When services are held, the chanting of the monks can be
heard coming from the delicately carved chapels which
house sacred statues. All the bonzes wear the same
orange robe and have the same shaven heads, looking as
though they have been mass-produced by their Creator.
Most of the temples are masterpieces of Siamese art and
architecture, notably the Phra Singh Wat, the temple of the
Lion Buddha, with its arched nagas; the Chiang Man Wat,
whose chedi is supported by fifteen elephantine cariatids;
and the Chedi Chet Yod Wat, modelled on a pagan temple,
whose chedi has seven slender spires.

One passes without transition from the sacred to the
profane. Chieng Mai has always kept alive a tradition of
high quality craftsmanship, and is the wellspring of Thai
creativity. Most of the craftwares sold in Bangkok are
made in Chieng Mai.

Chieng Mai is the capital of traditional Thai hand crafts. The above photos show the manufacture of a lacquer vase, the decoration of a carved wood panel, and the preparation of parasol ribs. Lacquer is derived from a resin gathered in the regions adjoining the frontier with Burma.

In former days, the different crafts were concentrated in different neighbourhoods or villages. With the proliferation of shops catering for tourists, this partitioning is less marked, but the secrets of manufacture are still passed down from father to son, and patience is still the prime virtue. In the vicinity of Wua Lai Road, the sound of rhythmic hammering announces the presence of the corporation of silversmiths. Their creations, shining like mirrors, are piled in the well-stocked shops: betel tins, offertory bowls, cups, bracelets, pendants, belts... objects far beyond the means of the humble worker who toils ten hours a day at the forge.

Continuing Southwards, one comes to the makers of laquerware. Lacquer is a resin gathered from trees by the Karens. It takes several months to fashion an object using traditional techniques. The teak or wickerwork base receives nine or ten successive coats of lacquer before it is perfectly varnished.

Above left: Parasols have an honorific significance. When they are superposed, there is always an odd number of them. Here they surround the chedi of the Phra That Doi Suthep Wat in Chieng Mai.

Opposite: A little Meo girl striking the gongs of a wat in Chieng Mai. She belongs to a non-Buddhist animist tribe.

Above right: Buddhists never enter a temple without making an offering of gold leaf, flowers, candles or incense sticks.

Those who prefer high-yield production are better advised to become weavers; with experience, it is possible to produce up to 6 metres of cloth a day. Cotton and silk are woven on the same looms that the girls of San Kamphaeng have used for the past hundred years or so.

On the outskirts of the city is Bo Sang, a village of parasol makers which owes its prosperity to an act of kindness on the part of a family man who one day encountered a monk whose parasol was broken, and offered to repair it. He had little experience but a generous disposition. With the help of his family, he made a new parasol for the monk. It was the birth of a craft industry; nowadays all the inhabitants of the village are parasol makers. Each person has his speciality: shaping the bamboo ribs, preparing the paper, and assembling and decorating the whole. Here again, patience is a virtue.

Night life in Chieng Mai is comparatively tame. The evening begins with the night bazaar in Changklan Road, offering such varied merchandise as cage-birds, Yao embroideries, opium pipes and chest expanders. The traders have got fed up with erecting and dismantling their stalls, and the market has now become a shopping centre, with nothing folkloric about it; but it is a bright and lively place, and one can even dine simply there on soup and skewered meat.

93

Or you may prefer to sample khan toke, a typical dish of Northern Thailand, which takes its name from the large tray with legs on which the food is served. One eats seated on the floor; the dishes are tasty and pleasantly spiced, accompanied by sticky rice balls dipped into various sauces.

A visit to a massage parlour is not a customary way of rounding off the evening; in this region, such establishments are traditionally more vigorous than erotic. One simply sips a glass of Mekong beside the River Ping, listening to guitar music that has nothing Thai about it.

Left: This young Meo boy is proud of his tame parrot, which he hopes to sell in the Chieng Mai market.

Right: The typical decoration of this temple in the North is highly detailed, with its two-toned varnished tiles, glass-incrusted nagas and chased wood panels.

The mountain tribes

*T*he air is mild, stirred by a light breeze. The mountain peaks shimmer in a white, mauve and purple haze. Nobody seems in a hurry to gather the pretty flowers, whose petals fall after a few weeks, leaving an oblong capsule whose contents are worth their weight in gold. For the flowers in question are opium poppies, which grow like weeds on the frontiers of Thailand, Laos and Burma.

Long-abandoned royal lands, the mountains were left free for anyone who wished to live there. They became the home of tribes from central China whose history dates back 4,000 years. Hmongs and Karens, Yaos and Lisus, Lahus and Akhas came in and settled there, leaving the valleys of the Yunnan in the hope of finding more fertile soil. Their migration was also the result of the practice of burning the vegetation to clear ground for cultivation, which exhausts the soil and destroys the forests.

They began to arrive in Thailand amid the confusion which reigned in the frontier area of the Golden Triangle at the beginning of the present century. They probably crossed the theoretical frontiers between the various countries without even noticing that they had done so, driven by the need to live above an altitude of 1,000 metres because of the fear of malaria.

The locations of their settlements are not clearly mapped, with villages moving every five or six years and new settlers ceaselessly arriving despite frontier controls.

With a few exceptions, these mountain tribes live in isolation, with little contact even between one tribe and another. Each tribe lives according to its own traditions, going about its own business. One of their activities is growing poppies, and the Thai government, under pressure from the international community, is seeking ways of enabling them to make a decent living by legal means.

After a few days spent walking among these wild mountains whose undulating horizon stretches as far as the eye can see, one begins to understand why these peoples keep themselves to themselves as they do. A plume of blue smoke, seen from afar, indicates the proximity of a village. Until you reach it, there is no way of knowing whether you are going to encounter Lisus, Karens, Hmongs or Lahus.

Left: Women of the Yao tribe in everyday costume. As can be seen, the same uniform attire is worn at an early age.

Top: Though illegal, poppies are still grown in the Golden Triangle; but the fields are becoming increasingly inaccessible.

Above: A young Lisu woman shopping in the town nearest her village. For some years past, ethnic minorities have become more integrated in the Thai community.

Left: The children of the mountain tribes are accustomed to helping with family trasks. This little Meo girl is carrying a locally-made bag on her back.

Right: Karen women wear less colourful attire than other minorities in the North. This girl with a bill-hook is helping with work on the farm.

Perhaps you will encounter an Akha woman, who will regard you with undisguised curiosity; it is quite likely that she has never seen a European before, or even a Thai from the plain. She smokes a pipe, and her teeth are stained red from chewing betel. Her get-up would create a sensation in Silom Road in Bangkok: a low-waisted miniskirt

revealing the navel, a patchwork jacket, embroidered gaiters, and a conical hat decorated with coins and buttons and trimmed with monkey-fur dyed red. Her previous address was perhaps somewhere in Burma. There are nearly 30,000 Akhas living in the province of Chieng Rai, North of the River Kok. They are simple and uncouth in many respects, but they manage to make the most of life and to enjoy themselves by singing and dancing and organizing fêtes.

Female attire varies from one area to another, and serves to identify the origin of the wearer. It is impossible to confuse a Hmong with a Yao or a Lisu with a Karen. Judges of women's fashions would find it difficult to decide between a Yao woman attired in an embroidered indigo dress with a tunic edged with a bright red boa, a gracious Lisu in a multi-coloured smock and fancy gaiters, and a Hmong in a double-breasted midnight-blue jacket, embroidered apron and brightly coloured pleated skirt.

The sea is for the fish, the air is for the birds, the mountains are for the Hmongs, says an old dictum. The Hmongs, also known as the Meos, live on the uplands at an altitude of between 1,000 and 2,000 metres. Numbering nearly 150,000, they are Thailand's largest community of mountain-dwellers (there are an estimated 6 million of them altogether). They earn their living by farming and hunting; family status and prosperity are assessed in terms

Left: The Lisu villages are located on high ground, at an altitude of around 1,800 metres. The girls are very clothes-conscious, and like wearing heavy silver jewellery, including the combined necklace and earrings seen here.

Above: This Meo is gathering opium by incising the capsule which remains after the poppy has lost its petals. The thick sap which oozes out turns brown in contact with the air, and is boiled and made up into cakes of crude opium.

of the heavy silver necklaces worn by the women. They often go "into town" (i.e. the nearest Thai village) to do their shopping, and sometimes they venture further afield; many young people who have taken advantage of the educational facilities provided by the Government of Thailand have entered university.

But such exploits are rare among the mountain-dwellers as a whole. The Yaos, for example, have more modest ambitions; they are hard-working farmers, and all they ask is to find a fertile valley in which to grow rice. Over the past ten years or so they have tended to become more settled, less nomadic. A young man who does not earn a good living has to remain unmarried, for he has to pay the girl's parents several thousand bahts to indemnify them for the loss of their daughter.

The arrival of a stranger in the mountain villages, which are not accessible by roads passable for vehicles, is a major event. The inhabitants are usually friendly as well as curious.

Among the Lisus, the price of a bride is even higher — at least 10,000 bahts. And that is not the end of it; the womenfolk have expensive tastes in jewellery! The Lisus, of whom there are about 20,000 in Thailand, are greatly attached to their mountain environment, and have a predilection for defensive positions around 1,800 metres. The cultivation of poppies is their main source of income, and any money they can set aside is spent on jewellery for their womenfolk and on fêtes. The new year festivities last five or six days, during which the women wear their most impressive finery, there is much dancing, and rice-spirit flows like water.

The Karens, however, consider these pleasures futile. The women have a certain status; they inherit automatically from their husbands. People marry at a later age, and marriages are usually "arranged". The couple live with the wife's mother. The Karens are the only ethnic group among whom Baptist missionaries have encountered a degree of success in Thailand. They are skilled elephant trainers, and most of the men work in the State-owned teak forests in the neighbourhood of Mae Sariang. An estimated 80,000 to 150,000 Karens live in Thailand, as compared with two million across the frontier in Burma, which has been a Federated Union since 1948.

At a time when Thailand is seeking to assert itself as the fifth Dragon of Asia, the government is finding it increasingly difficult to cope with ethnic minorities. Eradicating the cultivation of poppies without causing them hardship and without antagonizing them is a tricky task.

Above: Birth control is not yet practiced among the mountain-dwelling minorities. Children are always welcomed joyfully, and they are very soon taken under the wing of their older brothers and sisters.

Right: This Yao grandmother has had the good fortune to come by a pair of spectacles for her needlework. Yeo embroideries, featuring tiny cross-stitches, are of extremely fine workmanship.

Yao women wear very sophisticated finery on high days and holidays. All the jewellery is in solid silver, and necklaces are worn on the back when there is no more room in front.

Right: This Akha girl is wearing a ceremonial headdress. The hat is an essential part of women's attire among the Akhas. In the case of married women, it is surmounted by a conical coif. Depending on how wealthy the family is, it is decorated with silver jewellery, pearls, or monkey-fur.

The pleasures of the beaches

With a coastline 2,613 kilometres long, Thailand is well endowed with beaches, some of them facing the Gulf of Siam to the East, others bordering the Andaman Sea to the West. Pattaya, for example, can rival Acapulco as an exotic resort spot frequented by pleasure-loving cosmopolitan vacationers, offering all kinds of water-sports and night life.

Those in search of less sophisticated pleasures can find them further South along the peninsula: long beaches of white sand fringed with coconut palms, lapped by crystal-clear waters and backed by natural parks lush with rare orchids and giant bamboos.

The series of beaches begins with Cha-Am, only 170 kilometres from Bangkok, ideal for a week-end stay. Not far away is Hua Hin, made fashionable by King Rama VII in the nineteen twenties and still favoured by the royal court. Here, in contrast to Pattaya, are to be found peace and quiet, beauty and serenity. Continuing Southwards one comes to Prachuab Kirikhan, where those in search of solitude can find it in luxuriously appointed bungalows facing the sea.

Outside the major resort spots, the beaches of the South are the domains of fishermen, vendors of swallows' nests, oyster-pearl cultivators, turtle breeders and coconut growers. Like the rice cycle, fishing makes relentless demands on those who depend on it for their livelihood. The fishermen are at the mercy of the seasons, the currents and the weather. They go out at night to the deep off-shore waters, bringing back their catch at dawn.

Left: Three monks in a fraternal embrace resist the temptation to bathe on one of the innumerable beaches of Southern Thailand.

Top right: A fisherman prepares to land on the shore of Koh Samui, a paradisical island in the Gulf of Siam frequented by those in search of palm-fringed beaches.

The presence of Islam

*A*s one proceeds Southwards, Thailand merges imperceptibly with Malaysia; Buddhism gives way to the religion of Islam, and pagodas are replaced by mosques.

Introduced in the fifteenth century by merchants and marabouts from the Middle East, the Islamic faith spread and flourished in a more liberal form than in its lands of origin, with women enjoying greater freedom.

There are about 800,000 Islamic Thais of the Sunnite sect, 85% of them concentrated in the provinces of Yala, Narathiwat, Pattani, Trang, Krabi and Songkhla. Though of Thai nationality, they are culturally oriented towards Malaysia, and Radio Kuala Lumpur has more listeners among them than Radio Bangkok. But the Thais are tolerant by nature, and have never sought either to convert or to exclude the Muslims who live in the kingdom. The King has even had a palace built in Narathiwat as a reminder of the obligation of national unity.

In any event, the Islamic faith is firmly established in the peninsula. The Islamic religious leaders (orang baik), turbanned or wearing the traditional velvet cap, ensure that the faithful observe their religion as it is practiced in this part of the world, including praying, fasting, reading the Koran and observing Muslim fête days. Couples are married by the Imam, and their children, duly circumcised, attend Koranic schools. At birth, they are given the name of one of the twenty-five prophets of Mohammed. They dream of one day making the pilgrimage to Mecca, the high point in the life of every good Muslim.

Life in the kampong is centred around three main activities: fishing, rice growing and working in the hevea plantations. When the fishing craft (called in Malay prahu kolek) return with their catch it is often a Chinese who loads it aboard his truck to sell it in the town. Seasonal workers employed in the extensive hevea plantations turn up in their *song teo* (trucks which serve as collective taxis) indifferent to the world price of rubber on which their destiny depends. Only the older people remember with nostalgia the old days when evening entertainment was provided by the *talung*, the shadow theatre operator, now supplanted by the greatest revolution that has ever swept over the kampongs: the advent of television.

Left: Harvesting coconuts is the main occupation of the inhabitants of the island of Samui. The pulp is used as a culinary ingredient and in the cosmetics industry, the tree-trunk in the building industry, and the palm leaves for roofing and matting.

Right: This monkey wears a bell on its collar to signal its position to its master. The monkeys leap from one coconut tree to another without climbing down each time.

The coconut growers have facilitated their lives by training monkeys to gather their coconuts. The island of Samui is a prime example. It is part of an archipelago of 80 islands and islets in the South China Sea opposite Surat Thani, 677 kilometres from Bangkok. Before the spot became a vacation paradise, it was the kingdom's foremost supplier of coconuts. The monkeys are taught to climb the highest tree, select the mature coconuts, and throw them to the ground without braining passers-by (though one is well advised, in the picking season, to cast an upward glance). The monkeys of Samui supply Bangkok with two million coconuts a month.

Vaunted as the "pearl of the South" by glossy tourist brochures, Phuket is Thailand's largest island, lying in the Andaman Sea. It was prosperous long before the age of tourism; as long ago as the seventeenth century, the Dutch realized the value of its pearls — and of its tin ore, which was exploited in open-cast workings by Chinese labourers on the site of the present town of Phuket. Like Malaysia, the island also profited from the miraculous seed of Hevea, introduced experimentally by the Director ot the Botanic Gardens of Singapore in 1877.

The contrast between the "civilized" and the wild parts of Phuket is striking. On the one hand are coconut palms, rice paddies, cathedral-like hevea forests, and islets lapped by crystal-clear waters peopled with multi-coloured fish; on the other, sea-green marshes where lianas and mangroves proliferate among strangely shaped limestone rocks. The island is well endowed with tourist accommodation, including hotels in the international class and palm-thatched bungalows.

With its extensive beaches of white sand, its innumerable creeks and its tropical vegetation, Phuket is an exotic paradise. The gay and friendly people who live there add to its charm.

Following page: This rock in the bay of Pang Nga owes its celebrity to a scene in a James Bond film which was shot on this spot. It is now known as "James Bond Island".

The passion for cock-fighting

*I*n Asia, gambling is inseparable from all spectator sports, from boxing matches to combats between snakes and mongooses. Cock-fights are no exception. Samui is Thailand's major cock-fighting centre. Big money is involved; a champion bird can be worth up to 100,000 bahts — nearly three times the annual salary of a schoolteacher.

The young cocks are fed on rich and nourishing food — vitaminized cereals, rice-cakes, termites, ants eggs and crickets. They are massaged with saffron oil and washed several times a day to keep their temperature down to about 43°C.

During the fight, each cock is attended by its "doctor", ready to intervene if necessary. The cock must have endurance, for the fight comprises ten 15-minute rounds with a 10-minute pause between rounds. It is not necessarily a fight to the death, although in the South their spurs are sharpened. Magical forces are believed to decide the outcome.

Villagers of Koh Samui present their champions prior to a cock-fight. The spectators are exclusively men. Cock-fighting is taken very seriously, and bets can reach high figures.

Left: Large sailing junks are becoming increasingly rare in the China Sea. Some of them have been converted to exotic cruise ships for tourists.

Above: The bay of Pang Nga, dotted with hundreds of steep limestone rocks, is one of the most spectacular sights in Thailand. It has been compared to the bay of Halong.

When you tire of lounging on the beaches, you can take a cruise aboard a motor-boat around the bay of Pang Nga, dotted with hundreds of rocky islets of fantastic shapes. It was here that one of the episodes in a James Bond film was shot. After the trip you can savour a meal of fricassée crab flavoured with pimento and citronella in the village of Koh Pannyi, in the shadow of its mosque.

Further South is Koh Phi Phi, a coral-ringed island off Krabi. The island is a venue of sea-swallows, whose nests are an Asiatic culinary delicacy, the equivalent of caviar in the West. The islanders climb bamboos to collect the nests at a height of more than 15 metres. It is no doubt worth the effort, for if we are to believe Paul Morand swallows' nests are even more nutritious than Tiger Balm: "as saturated with iodine as kelp, as salty as sea-water, as rich in phosphorus as fish, this laboriously fashioned work of the swallow is a restorative for jaded appetites".

Koh Phi Phi also boasts magnificent natural scenery, as well as golden beaches lapped by pale blue waters; a precarious miracle for present-day Robinson Crusoes — too good to be true!

A little boy frees a bird to acquire merit in a future life. Cage birds are sold in the vicinity of the temples.

Patrick de Wilde uses Nikon photographic equipment and Kodak film.

Our thanks are due to the Thailand National Tourist Office for its help in the production of this book.